TWO CON

Comprising

WHY I LEFT THE CHURCH OF ENGLAND

James Britten

1893

THE ESSENTIALS OF SPIRITUAL UNITY

Ronald Knox

1918

CATHOLIC TRUTH SOCIETY

PUBLISHERS TO THE HOLY SEE

The absence of authority and of definite teaching – these were the reasons which induced me to leave the Church of England.

James Britten (1846-1924), an eminent botanist, was co-founder of CTS; Ronald Knox (1888-1957) the most famous priest-convert of the 20th century.

CTS ONEFIFTIES

Originally published as *Why I Left the Church of England*, 1893;
reprinted as *The Conversion of James Britten*, 1931;
The Essentials of Spiritual Unity, 1918.
Published by The Incorporated Catholic Truth Society,
40-46 Harleyford Road, London SE11 5AY
www.ctsbooks.org
ISBN 978 1 78469 543 9

THE CONVERSION OF JAMES BRITTEN

James Britten

THE CONVERSION OF
JAMES BRITTEN, K.C.S.G.,[1]

FOUNDER OF THE CATHOLIC TRUTH SOCIETY

I wish to begin this lecture with an apology. No one can be better aware than I am that, except to one person—myself—the reasons which impel me to any course of action are of the very slightest importance—or rather, of no importance at all. This lecture is, like others of our course, the sequence of one delivered lately in this neighbourhood in connection with the Protestant Alliance: the title is an adaptation of that adopted on the former occasion; and the fact that up and down the country, various people, including more or less escaped nuns and others, are telling audiences—sometimes large ones—why they "left the Church of Rome," seems to show that the experiences of what used to be called 'verts are still attractive.

The reasons which people allege for leaving one communion and joining another are very serious, and sometimes very curious. Mr. Fitzgerald, for example, said he became a Protestant because of the ignorance of the Catholic clergy and the worship of images. Well, as to ignorance, those who heard Mr. Fitzgerald will agree with me in thinking that he is hardly a competent judge; and as to the worship of images—supposing for one moment, what every Catholic will resent as an impossibility, that Catholics fell into so gross a sin—I would remark

---

[1] [A Lecture delivered in March, 1893, in St. George's School, Southwark, in answer to one given by a Mr. Fitzgerald, of the Protestant Alliance. The date of the lecture must be borne in mind by the readers of the pamphlet, which, save for a footnote on p. 20, is reprinted without alteration.]

that the Jewish people more than once did the same, without thereby ceasing to be the people of God. Another Protestant lecturer was so shocked by the definition of Papal Infallibility in 1870, that she—at once left the Church? Oh dear no! remained in it for eighteen years, and then withdrew. A Nonconformist friend of mine told me the other day that his sister had joined the Church of England. "You see," he said, "she is a wise woman. She told me she found that if her daughters were to mix in the best society, they must be Church people, so she and her husband joined the Establishment." Another friend, who had been a Baptist all his life, suddenly joined the Established Church. "The fact of it was," he said to me, "they were always quarrelling at the chapel, so one day I said I'd had enough of it, and I took the girls off to church—and now I've had them confirmed there, and we like it." I do not think these were good reasons for changing one's belief; my object, however, is not to criticize other people's reasons, but to give you my own, and this I will proceed to do without further delay.

One thing only I will add—an assurance that I am most anxious to avoid anything which can in any way hurt the feelings of those who differ from me. I have no reason, indeed, for speaking harshly or disrespectfully of the Church of England. To one section of it I owe my training in many Catholic doctrines, while to another section I am indebted for having opened my eyes to the fact that these doctrines were not the doctrines of the Church of England. You will hear from me no attacks upon the character of the Anglican clergy, not only because I believe them to be an excellent body of men, but because, even if they were not so, their personal shortcomings would no more invalidate their teachings than the character of Balaam invalidated the truth of his prophetic utterances. It would, I think, be well if some Protestant lecturers would bear this in mind, just as they might remember that a Church which could claim the allegiance of a Newman and a Manning is hardly likely to be as corrupt or as ignorant as they would have their hearers suppose.

From my earliest days, I was brought up at St. Barnabas', Pimlico—one of the churches most intimately associated with the growth of the High Church views in London. It was opened in 1850, and among those who preached on the occasion was the late Cardinal (then Archdeacon) Manning. In 1851 the Protestant feeling of a certain section of the community was roused. The riots which from time to time have disgraced the Protestant party—which, nevertheless, claims toleration as one of its virtues—and which culminated some years later in the scandalous scenes at St. George's in the East, broke out here. The timid Bishop of London closed the church and caused the resignation of Mr. Bennett, who received the living of Frome Selwood, Somerset, where he died some few years since, deeply regretted by his flock, whom he had familiarized with almost every Catholic doctrine and practice. It is worth noting, as showing the marvellous stride which Ritualism has made in the last forty years, that at St. Barnabas' the only then unusual ornaments were a plain cross and two candles on the Holy Table; an oak screen before the chancel, surmounted by a cross; a surpliced choir; and a service modelled on that of the English cathedrals.[1] No vestments save the ordinary surplice and black stole; no incense; no banners; no prayers save those in the Book of Common Prayer. The ornaments of the church, which forty years ago had to be closed to protect it from the mob, would now hardly excite the notice of the Church Association.

My own memory dates, I suppose, from somewhere about 1856. The two great waves of conversion to the Catholic Church, which followed the secession of Newman in 1845 and Manning in 1851, had passed: and in spite of occasional Protestant outbursts, the effects of Protestant lectures, and the adverse judgements of Privy Councils and other bodies, the High Church movement was steadily and everywhere gaining ground.

I will as briefly as possible tell you what I was taught to believe. First I was taught that Our Lord founded a Church, which He had

---

[1] There was indeed, a stone altar, which was subsequently removed, but this being covered was not conspicuously different from an ordinary table.

built on the foundation of His Apostles, He Himself being the chief corner stone: that He had conferred on His Apostles certain powers by which they were enabled to carry on His work; that the Apostles had the power of forgiving sins, of consecrating the Eucharist, and of transmitting to their successors the supernatural power which they had themselves received: that the Apostles and those whom they consecrated were the rulers of the Christian Church: that this Church had power to define what was to be believed, and that it could not err, because of the promise of Christ that He would be with it, even to the end of the world: that the Church, moreover, was divinely guided in a very special manner by the Holy Ghost, and that its definitions to the end of time were inspired by the Holy Ghost, of whom Christ had said, "When He, the Spirit of Truth is come, He shall lead you into all truth": that the Church and not the Bible was God's appointed teacher: that the traditions of the Church were of equal authority with the Bible: and that the Church was the only authorized interpreter of the latter.

I was further taught that the grace of God was conveyed to the soul principally by means of the Sacraments, and that by Baptism the stain of original sin was removed. With regard to the Real Presence of Our Lord in the Holy Communion, I can best explain the teaching that I received by saying that I was never conscious of any change of belief when I became a Catholic. The books which I used as an Anglican I could use equally well as a Catholic; they were compiled almost exclusively from Catholic sources, and before ever I had entered a Catholic church or read a Catholic book, I was familiar with the wonderful eucharistic hymns of St. Thomas, and the other doctrinal hymns, modern as well as ancient, of the Catholic Church.

I do not think that in those days we were taught, as Anglicans are taught now, that there were seven Sacraments, but the practical result was the same. I shall never forget the care with which I was prepared for Confirmation; it never occurred to me to doubt that the clergy had the power of forgiving sins; indeed, I think I exaggerated this power, for I thought that the declaration of absolution at Matins and Evensong was sacramental. Confession was not urged as it is now, and confessionals were not, as they are now, openly placed in the churches; but in sermons and in private instruction the "benefit of absolution" as the Prayer-book calls it, was referred to, and we knew that confessions were heard in the sacristy. I have already said that we believed in the apostolic succession—in other words, in the Sacrament of Orders; and it was difficult to ignore the plain command of St. James as to Extreme Unction—indeed, I have never been able to understand, save on the basis of Luther's well-known saying that the Epistle of James was "a matter of straw," how Protestants evade compliance with this text.

As to externals, although in those days these had developed but little, the principle of them was laid down. We were told—and I do not see how any one can deny it—that there were two rituals authorized by Almighty God—the ancient Jewish rite, and the mystical vision of the Apocalypse. In both were found the symbolic use of vestments and incense, music and ceremonial: nowhere did we find any indication that these externals were to be done away, and we know that the Christian Church adopted them from as early a period as was possible. The English Church, indeed, was shorn of her splendour, but the time would come when she would arise and put on her beautiful garments; and if there should be any High Churchman among my hearers, he will say, and say truly, that that time *has* come, and that, so far as externals go, the Established Church can now vie successfully with the Roman ritual in splendour and dignity.

And as with other externals so with music. Among the many things for which I am grateful to those who brought me up, few are more present to me than the love which they gave me for the old plain chant of the Church—the chant which we called Gregorian, thereby giving honours to the great Pope who sent St. Augustine to bring this nation unto God. And with the old chants we had the old words—not only the Psalms of David, but the words of the Fathers of the Church in her hymns—of St. Ambrose, and St. Gregory, and St. Bede, and

St. Thomas Aquinas: for in those early days not a hymn was sung in that church which had not upon it the hall-mark of antiquity.

To the same hand which translated most of these hymns into sonorous and manly English, I owed my knowledge of the lives of the Saints, as portrayed in the volumes setting forth the "Triumphs of the Cross" and the "Followers of the Lord." To Dr. Neale—that great liturgical scholar—I shall always feel a debt of gratitude for having made me understand, however imperfectly, what is meant by the Communion of Saints, and for having brought to my knowledge that wonderful storehouse of saintly history which is among the many treasures of the Catholic Church. It is true that we did not then, as Anglicans do now, invoke them, or address our litanies to the Mother of God; yet the veneration of the Blessed Virgin and the Saints was inculcated upon us in many ways.

So with the observance not only of festivals, but of fasts—the duty of keeping both was impressed on us. The brightness of the sanctuary, with its many lights and flowers, and the stately procession chanting psalms, were associated with all the great Christian festivals, making "the beauty of holiness" something more than a name; while the times of self-denial and the penitential season of Lent were brought home to us by the silent organ and the violet-hung sanctuary. The duty of supporting our pastors, the equality of all men before God,

> "Who has but one same death for a hind,
>
> And one same death for a king,"

were also taught us, as fully as the Church herself teaches them.

You may wonder what were the impressions I received with regard to the Catholic Church on one side, and Nonconformists on the other. With regard to the Church I was taught that there were three branches—the Anglican, the Greek and the Roman—and that of these three the Catholic Church was made up: that in this country the Church of England represented the Catholic Church, and that the

Roman branch had no business here—though I am thankful to say that I cannot remember ever having heard at St. Barnabas' a single sermon against Roman Catholics, or an uncharitable word regarding them. I therefore had none of those prejudices which seem inseparable from certain forms of Protestantism—prejudices which prevent even a fair hearing of the Catholic position. I remember one sermon on the honour due to the Blessed Virgin, in which the Roman devotion to her was spoken of as excessive; and another on St. Peter, in which his primacy as distinct from her supremacy was acknowledged; but until I was seventeen I never heard the Protestant side of the Church of England advanced from any pulpit, although then, as now, the itinerant Protestant lecturer presented to those who were credulous enough to accept his statements a caricature of the Catholic Church. In those days a Mr. Edward Harper, who had some prominent position in the Orange Society, occupied the place which is now held by Mr. Collette, and was filled, until lately, by Mr. Mark Knowles.

I ought to add that I had never attended a Roman Catholic service, and had only once entered a Catholic church. This was the old Oratory, into which I went one winter afternoon on my way to the South Kensington Museum. One of the few things I knew about what I considered the Roman branch of the Church, was that the Blessed Sacrament was reserved on its altars, and I remember kneeling in the dark, flat-roofed Oratory, with its lamp burning before the altar, in adoration of the Presence which I felt to be there. I was quite sure—for I had never heard it called in question—that the views I have given were those of the Church of England: that the Reformation, disastrous as it was in many ways, had not broken the apostolic succession: and that the Western and Eastern Churches, equally with the Anglican, had Orders and Sacraments, and were of the unity of the Faith.

With Nonconformists it was different. They had no authorized ministry, and therefore no Sacraments. They had thrown off the authority of the Church, and substituted their own interpretation of the Bible. They were the followers of Korah, Dathan, and Abiram;

against them was directed the warning, "Mark those who cause divisions among you, and avoid them." I am afraid that we looked upon them as socially inferior to ourselves—certainly as people to be avoided—and as "Protestants," a term which even then Anglicans held in contempt. With Catholics we had much in common—indeed, we *were* Catholic ourselves: but Dissent, with its numberless divisions, absence of dignity, unauthorized teachers, and ugly conventicles, was far from us, and with it we could hold no communion.

This was my position, until, at about the age of eighteen, I went into the country to study medicine. I shall never forget my first Sunday there. There was a magnificent old parish church, with deep chancel and broad aisles, choked up with pews of obstructive design. A small table with a shabby red cloth stood away under the picture which concealed the east window; a choir of a handful of men and boys, unsurpliced and untidy, sang the slender allowance of music; a parish clerk responded for the congregation;—these were the objects that met my eyes and ears that first Sunday of my exile. But that was not all. We had a sermon delivered by a preacher in a black gown—to me a new and hideous vestment—on behalf of the Sunday-schools. That sermon I shall always remember. In the course of it, the preacher enumerated the things they did *not* teach the children in the schools: they did *not* teach them they were born again in baptism, they did *not* teach that the clergy were descended from the Apostles, they did *not* teach that they had power to forgive sins, they did *not* teach a real presence in the Communion—"Real *presence!*" I heard a parson say in that church: "I believe in a real *absence!*"—they did not teach the doctrine of good works. I began to wonder what was left to be taught, until the preacher explained that predestination and salvation by faith alone were inculcated upon the children. On the next Sunday the Holy Communion was administered—*how*, I can hardly describe, except by saying that it was manifest that no belief in its supernatural aspect was maintained. I can see now the parish clerk at the end of the service, walking up the chancel, and the minister coming towards him with the paten in one hand and the chalice in the other, waiting, while he, standing, ate and drank the contents of each.

My first feeling was that these clergy had no right or place in the Church of England. There was a moderately "high" church five miles off, and whenever I could, I found my way there. But it became unpleasantly plain that the Church of England, which I had regarded as an infallible guide, spoke with two voices:—I began to realize that even on vital matters two diametrically opposed opinions not only *could be*, but *were*, held and preached. I knew my Book of Common Prayer and its rubrics as well as I knew my Bible; but to one part of it my attention had never been called, as it now was Sunday by Sunday. I had known without realizing all that it implied, that the Queen was, in some way, the Head of the Church—or rather, of two churches, one in England and one in Scotland: but I now found that she declared herself to be "Supreme Governor of the Church of England, and by God's ordinance, Defender of the Faith": that General Councils, which I had been taught to believe infallible, could not be held "without the commandment and will of princes," and "may err, and sometimes have erred, in things pertaining unto God": that Confirmation, Penance, and the like, were not Sacraments of the Gospel: that the benefits of Baptism were "confined to them that receive it rightly": that the reception of the Body of Christ in the Holy Communion is dependent on the faith of the recipient: and that "the sacrifices of Masses…were blasphemous fables and dangerous deceits." This last was indeed a trial to me. It is true that twenty-five years ago the word "Mass" was not in common use among Anglicans as it is now, and I do not think an Anglican clergyman would have been found to say in public, as one said the other day, that "he would not stay a minute in a church where the Mass was not, for if they had not got the Mass, they had no worship whatever." But we knew that the term was retained in the first reformed Prayer-book, and that it was the name employed throughout the Western Church for the Eucharistic service.

Here then was my difficulty: and the more I faced it the more

I found that the ground which I had thought so sure was slipping away from under me. Not, thank God, that I ever doubted any of the truths which had been implanted in me: but I began to see, more and more clearly, that the authority on which I had thought them to rest was altogether lacking. I found that what I had received as the teaching of a Church, was only the teaching of a certain section of its clergy, and that other clergy, with exactly as much authority, taught directly opposite opinions: they were not priests, they said: they claimed to offer no sacrifice; no office of forgiving sins was theirs; they possessed no supernatural powers.

This was bad enough, but there was worse behind. The other branches of the Church—what did they say on these momentous points? Alas! there was no room for doubt here. Neither the Eastern nor Western "branches," each of them far larger than the Anglican, would admit for a moment the claims of the Anglican clergy to be priests: and a large section of themselves equally denied it. The bishops in some cases expressly told the candidates for ordination that they were not made priests; and if there were no priests, how could the sacraments depending on them be celebrated? It was no special ill-will to Anglicans that Rome showed by refusing to recognize their orders; for she never denied those of the Greeks, although these were equally separated from her unity. The Branch Theory broke down—it would not work.

Then I read other books, many of them by Newman, for whom Anglicans in those days cherished a warm affection and respect in spite of his secession. And more and more the conviction was forced upon me that I had received the beliefs in which I had been brought up on the authority of certain individual members of a body which not only tolerated, but taught with equal authority the exact opposite of these beliefs—that the Anglican Communion, even as represented by those who claimed for it Catholicity, was a mere Protestant sect, differing only from more recent denominations in that it retained certain shreds and patches of the old faith. It was, in short, a compromise—a *via media* between Rome and Dissent—and it was as unsatisfactory as compromises usually are.

Meanwhile there came upon me more and more plainly the claims of a Church which taught with authority all that I believed; which claimed to be the one body having a right to teach; and which, without equivocation or hesitation, pointed out to its members one only means of salvation. By one of those occurrences which we call accidents I became aquainted with a Catholic priest—one of the first of these Anglicans who gave up friends and position and everything that could make life happy at the call of their Master. From him I learned what was hitherto lacking to my knowledge of the Church; I realized, as I had never done before, that the first mark of God's Church was unity—a mark which no one can pretend to find in the Church of England: and after a period of anxiety such as none can know who have not experienced it, I was received into that unity.

Of my experience since, you will not expect me to speak. If I must say anything, I will venture to employ the words of Cardinal Newman, which express better than any words of mine could, my feelings now:—"From the day I became a Catholic to this day, I have never had a moment's misgiving that the Communion of Rome is the Church which the Apostles set up at Pentecost, which alone has 'the adoption of sons, and the glory, and the covenants, and the revealed law, and the service of God, and the promises,' and in which the Anglican Communion whatever its merits and demerits, whatever the great excellence of individuals in it, has, as such, no part. Nor have I ever for a moment hesitated in my conviction that it was my duty to join the Catholic Church, which in my own conscience I felt to be divine."

When I had told the friends with whom I was living that I had become a Catholic, the result somewhat astonished me: and those good Protestants who assume—as many do—that persecution and Popery are inseparably connected, while Protestantism and liberty of conscience are convertible terms, may like to know what happened.

15

My desk was broken open; my private letters were stolen; letters sent me through the post were intercepted, opened, and sometimes detained; I was prevented from going to a Catholic church and from seeing a Catholic priest; a picture of the Crucifixion which I had had in my room for years, was profaned in a way which I do not care to characterize. These things are small and trifling compared with what many have suffered, but what light do not even they throw upon that right of private judgement which Protestants profess to hold so dear!

One thing which seemed to me at my conversion remarkable still remains to me one of the most wonderful features of Protestantism— the universal assumption that Catholics do not know what they themselves believe, and that Protestants understand it far better. The average Protestant for instance, thinks and often asserts that we believe that the Pope cannot sin, that we worship images, that we are disloyal to the Crown, that we put Our Lady in the place of God, that we sell absolution for money and have a recognized tariff for the remission of sins, that we may not read the Bible, that we would burn every Protestant if we could, that we lie habitually, that our convents are haunts of vice, that our priests are knaves or conscience imposters, and that our laity are dupes or fools—I could, if time would allow, easily bring extracts from Protestant writers in support of each of these positions. Not only so, but—by isolated texts of Scripture; by scraps of the Fathers, torn from their context, and often mistranslated; by misrepresentation of history; by fragments of prayers and hymns, interpreted as no Catholic would interpret them; by erroneous explanations of what they see in our churches; by baseless inferences arising from ignorance of the very language we use—they formulate and are not ashamed to propagate charges against us which in many cases we cannot condemn seriously, because it is impossible to help laughing at them. Our contradictions are not listened to; our corrections are unheeded; our statements are disbelieved. "Give us," we say, "at least fair play; hear what we have to say for ourselves; do not condemn us unheard; do not assume that we are all fools and rogues." But we are not listened to: we are not allowed to know what we ourselves believe! "Oh for the rarity of Christian charity," or at any rate of Protestant charity. We are sometimes accused of omitting one of the commandments: but it is the bigoted Protestant who does this—he entirely forgets that there is in the Decalogue one which says sternly—"Thou shalt not bear false witness against thy neighbour." How many Protestants who speak against the Church have ever expended a penny on the Catechism which contains a full, clear statement of Christian Doctrine, which is approved by authority, and on which the religious education of our children is based? Yet they would learn more from it of what we really believe than from every tract in Mr. Kensit's shop, or from all the books which Mr. Collette ever wrote.

It often puzzles me how it is that Protestants do not realize the utter futility of the attempts they have been making for the last fifty years to arrest the tide of Catholic tendency which is flooding the nation. Go into St. Paul's—say on the festival of the Gregorian Association—see the long procession of surpliced choirs with their banners, many of them bearing Catholic devices: listen to the old antiphons, unauthorized indeed by the Book of Common Prayer, set to the chants to which they are sung in the Church throughout the world wherever the Divine Office is chanted; see the preacher mount the pulpit prefacing his sermon with the invocation of the Blessed Trinity and the sign of the Cross; hear him refer, as one referred two years since, to "Our Lady"—a title only less dear to Catholics than that of Our Lord: and as you sit and listen, look to the end of the church, with its dignified and decorated altar and the gorgeous reredos, not unworthy of a Catholic church, with the great crucifix in its centre and over all the statue of Mary with her Divine Child in her arms; and as you leave the church, do not forget to notice the side chapel and its handsome altar, with cross, and flowers and lights, where the daily communion service is held. Then remember that less than forty years since, not one of those ornaments or signs could be seen in the desolate, dirty edifice, with its shabby communion table well-nigh out of sight under the east window. Go to Westminster, and see, prominent at the restored north door, another statue of Mary with her Child. Go up and down the country, both to your large towns and to your remote villages, and you will find the same advance—only more developed. Last year I strolled into the magnificent old abbey church of a little Oxfordshire village: the air was dim and heavy with incense, there were three altars, each duly furnished with lights, cross, and sacring-bell; on the notice board was a copy of the parish magazine, in which I read an exhortation on the duty of hearing Mass on Sundays which might have been taken—and perhaps was taken—from a Catholic manual of instruction: and a list of the services to be held on the feast of Corpus Christi! The crucifix is now common in Protestant churches; pictures of Our Lady are not rare; statues of her are to be found—why do not our Protestant friends look to this, instead of raising their voices against Catholicism? They shriek and rant after their manner; yet one stronghold after another is captured, and they stand by and are powerless to hinder it.

Look at the wealth of literature of every kind, which pours forth from the ritualistic press; the manuals and treatises, the dogmatic works, the numberless little books, each more advanced than the last, with which the country is literally flooded, and of which the St. Agatha's Sunday Scholars' Book, which lately received a notice from the Protestant Alliance, is but one out of a thousand. Look even at the levelling up which has marked the publications of so eminently respectable a body as the Society for Promoting Christian Knowledge. How is it that, with all your power and influence and money, you cannot arrest this advance in the direction of Rome?

And what about Rome itself? There are those who think that England is rapidly becoming Catholic. I am not of that number, but I cannot fail to see that the fields are white unto harvest, and I see too that the labourers are being sent forth into the harvest.

More than fifty years ago, Macaulay pointed out, in that wonderful essay on Ranke's History of the Popes which I would commend to all Protestants who do not know it, as a "most remarkable fact, that no Christian nation which did not adopt the principles of the Reformation before the end of the 16th century, should ever have adopted them. Catholic communities have since that time become infidel and become Catholic again: but none has become Protestant." How is it at home? Protestants have poured money into Ireland: they did not scruple to avail themselves, to their everlasting disgrace, of the sufferings of the great famine in order to buy over with their funds the souls and bodies of the destitute Irish. "God has opened a great door to us in Ireland"— such was the blasphemous announcement which prefaced one of the appeals for those liberal funds without which no Protestant missionary enterprise, at home or abroad, can be carried on. What is the result? Is Ireland less Catholic than she was? Come closer—come to England— here are facts which Protestants will not dispute, for they will come to you with the authority of the Protestant Alliance, from one of whose publications I quote them. Since 1851, the number of priests in England has more than trebled itself; of churches, chapels, and stations we have now 1,387, where in 1851 we had 586; of religious houses of men we have 220, against 17, forty years ago; of convents—those favourite objects of attack to a certain class of Protestants, those places whose inmates, to judge from the rubbish one hears and reads, have only one aim, to escape—we have just nine time as many as we had in 1851: the numbers are 450 and 53. Come nearer home: in 1851 the diocese of Southwark included what is now the diocese of Portsmouth; there were then in it 67 priests: there are now, in the two dioceses 428—an increase of 363: there were 57 churches and stations, where there are now exactly 200; there are 80 convents instead of 9: there are 38 monasteries instead of one! Come to these very doors; when I came to live in Southwark, eight years ago, there was for this vast district one church—the Cathedral—with four priests: now the staff at the Cathedral is more than doubled, and Walworth, the Borough and

Vauxhall are separated into distinct missions, each with two priests. Add to this such churches as St. Alphege and St. Agnes, where the doctrines taught, and the ornaments used are almost identical with our own; All Saints' (Lambeth), St. John the Divine, Christ Church (Clapham), and many more, where sacramental teaching of an advanced type is given: and then calculate for yourselves what effect in this neighbourhood the puny and impotent attacks of the Protestant Alliance are likely to produce: a society whose patron should surely be the good old lady who thought to sweep back the sea with a mop: whose members spend their money on red rags, and waste their time by shaking them in the face of a bull—I mean John Bull, who doesn't care twopence about them. My Protestant friends, there was one of old who gave sound advice to those who took counsel to slay Peter and they that were with him: "Refrain from these men, and let them alone: for if this counsel or this work be of men, it will come to naught; but if it be of God, ye cannot overthrow it; lest haply ye be found to fight against God." Remember that "in spite of dungeon, fire and sword,"—in spite of penal laws, which the Lord Chief Justice has lately styled "a code as hateful as anything ever seen since the foundation of the world"—the faith is among you still; the gates of hell have not prevailed against it.

And—speaking quite soberly and dispassionately—I do not hesitate to say that some of the weapons which are employed against the Church seem to me to come from within those gates. I respect the conscientious, God-fearing Protestants who, under the influence of strong delusion, feel it their duty to oppose the Church. I remember the case of Saul, afterwards called Paul, and how he persecuted the Church of God; and I do not despair of their conversion. I have only sympathy for those who are misled by prejudice and bigoted teachers. Every convert can say, with the man in the Gospel, "Whereas I was blind now I see"; and I am not sure that those who have had the happiness of being born Catholics always make sufficient allowance for the imperfect vision of those without the fold. But what shall be said in defence of those who are not ashamed to write and to publish calumnies, as foul as they are false, against priests and nuns, and the Sacraments of the Church—those "lewd fellows of the baser sort" who under the guise of religion, do not scruple to pander to the lowest and worst of passions by the circulation of filthy fictions of which "Maria Monk" is by no means the worst—of works which, so far as I know, are to be found in only two places in London—in the shop of a Protestant publisher, and in a street which has for years obtained an evil notoriety for the sale of indecent literature. I am not going to name these books: but if anyone is anxious, for any good purpose, to know to what I refer, I am ready to tell him. Some years since, one of the worst of these was seized and condemned as an indecent publication; since then, the Protestant purveyors[1] of pornographic publications have been more careful to keep within the letter of the law, although it is not long since the editor of *Truth*—by no means a scrupulous purist—denounced some of their wares as outraging decency. These and the highly spiced lectures "to men" or "to women *only*"—appeal to a certain class of persons; and I call upon all decent men and women, be they Jew, Turk, heretic, or infidel—and above all, upon Mr. Collette, who was at one time intimately connected with a body called the Society for the Suppression of Vice—to dissociate themselves from any part in the wholesale propagation of indecency which is carried on in the name of religion. The cause must indeed be a bad and a hopeless one which can stoop to avail itself of weapons such as these.

But I will not refer further to a hateful kind of warfare with which very few will sympathize. I will rather briefly apply to two among the many schools of thought in the Establishment the remarks which I have made.

To the Protestant or Low Churchman I would say: Can you conscientiously remain in a Church the members of which claim to hold all Roman doctrine, save that of submission to the Pope—which permits the teaching not only of Baptismal Regeneration and the Real

---

[1] See *Truth*, Dec. 28, 1893, for further remarks on one of these persons.

Presence, but of Confession, the Monastic or Religious Life, the use of Images, Fasting, Prayers and Masses for the Dead, the Invocation of Saints, Prayers to the Blessed Virgin, the power of dispensing from religious obligations; which not only allows these things to be taught, but permits them to be emphasized by every external adjunct? To the High Churchman my question is exactly the converse of this. You believe all or most of the points which I have just enumerated: can you remain in communion with those who deny them? Read, if you have not read it, a pamphlet on the Reformation by one of your own Bishops—Dr. Ryle—one of those whom you regard as successors of the Apostles, with the power of ordaining priests. He tells you how the reformers "stripped the office of the clergy of any sacerdotal character"—how they removed the words "sacrifice" and "altar" from the Prayer-book, and retained the word priest only in the sense of presbyter or elder—how they denied the power of the keys—how they cast out the Sacrifice of the Mass as a blasphemous fable, took down the altars, prohibited images and crucifixes, and "declared that the sovereign had supreme authority and chief power in this realm in all causes ecclesiastical." What is gained by the wearing of cope and mitre and the teaching of sacramental doctrine by one bishop, if another can at the same time, with equal authority, denounce all these things? and how can a Church with any claim to be considered as teaching with authority tolerate with equanimity both of these extremes?

We Catholics are so accustomed to the unity of the Church that we do not perhaps always think what a wonderful thing it is: and Protestants, I find, often do not realize it. They sometimes point to our religious Orders as if they were equivalent to their own manifold divisions! It is, I believe, the literal truth that, as the sun shines day by day on each part of the world, he sees at each moment the blessed Sacrifice of the Altar uplifted to the Eternal Father. Where, save in the Catholic Church, shall we find such a fulfilment of the prophecy "From the rising of the sun unto the going down of the same shall incense be offered to My Name and a pure offering"? Not only so, but throughout the world—from "Greenland's icy mountains" to "India's coral strand"—wherever two or three are gathered together in the One Name is the same belief, the same sacrifice, mainly the same ritual: so that the Irish exile leaving the Old World for the New, where Catholicism is increasing with rapid strides, is as much at home in the churches of New York as he was in his roadside country chapel in the old country. Can any Catholic for a moment conceive the possibility of finding any one doctrine preached at St. George's, contradicted by the priest at Walworth controverted in the sermon in the Catholic chapel at Vauxhall, and called in question by Canon Murnane in the Borough? Can he imagine Cardinal Vaughan's teaching on the Mass contradicted by our own beloved Bishop? But will any Protestant tell me that—to take the two Anglican churches nearest to us—the teaching at St. Paul's is identical with that at St. Alphege's? Could Mr. Allwork's congregation next Sunday avail themselves of Mr. Goulden's ministrations, or join in the hymns and prayers addressed to the Blessed Sacrament and the Mother of God?

The Catholic can go all over the world, and wherever he goes he will find the same Faith and the same Sacrifice. The Protestant cannot go at random into two churches in the same neighbourhood with any certainty that the teaching or ceremonial will be similar, and that with regard to the most vital points of faith. "How can two walk together except they be agreed?" Remember that, as the cowl does not make the monk, so the most elaborate ritual and the most advanced teaching cannot make a Catholic. A few weeks ago I strolled into a handsome church in this neighbourhood, just as a lady dressed like a nun was taking the school-children to service. There was the raised altar, with its flowers and lights and crucifix and what looked very like a tabernacle, and before the altar burned seven lamps. "Is this a Catholic Church?" I said to the verger. "No, sir, Church of England," was the reply. My friends, disguise it as you will, the truth will out: your Catholic church is only the Church of England after all.

One point more. When I was thinking of becoming a Catholic,

I pointed out to a friend these differences existing in the Church of England. Both, I said, cannot be true, but neither the Church herself, nor the State which supports her, is able to say with authority which is right. My friend told me—what I believe people still say—that High and Low Church were united in essentials. Surely the most ignorant and superstitious Papists ever invented by a Protestant lecturer would recoil before such an absurdity as this statement involves! Surely it is "essential" to know whether Baptism is a mere symbol or a regenerating sacrament; it cannot be a matter of indifference whether the sons of men have or have not the power on earth to forgive sins; it cannot be a matter of opinion whether the Sacrifice of the Mass is a blasphemous fable and dangerous deceit, or the renewal of the great Sacrifice offered on Calvary? There must be an authority to pronounce upon these points, and the Church of England neither has nor claims to be such authority. From the time of the Gorham Judgement, which left Baptism an open question, down to the Archbishop of Canterbury's decision the other day, uncertainty, vagueness, and indecision have marked every attempt to formulate any definite opinion. This last attempt has indeed justified ritualism on the ground that it means nothing in particular, and above all, nothing Roman. No wonder the *Times* spoke of a "sense of unreality" in "the effort to treat, as neutral or colourless, acts which we all know to be, in the view of a party in the Church, technical symbols and unequivocal doctrinal signs. It is true that, with marvellous effrontery, a popular Anglican hymn asserts—

> "We are not divided,
>
> All one body we;
>
> One in hope and doctrine,
>
> One in charity." [1]

---

[1] [It would appear that even Anglicans themselves have been struck by the absurdity of this statement, for in the new edition of *Hymns Ancient and Modern* the verse begins:
"Though divisions harass,
All one body we."]

But does an Anglican believe it to be true? "Not divided!" Is there any one who will assert that the "doctrine" preached in the first half-dozen Anglican churches he comes across will be "one"?—or that the teaching of what is termed, with unconscious irony, the "religious press," has any claims to be considered identical? If the "doctrine" is one, why do we find in the same Church two such organizations as the English Church Union and the Church Association, each diametrically opposed to the other, and the latter continually prosecuting the clergy who represent the views of the former? Is there anywhere such a spectacle of division as this—a division which, as soon as the bonds of State Establishment shall have been broken asunder, cannot fail to be even more manifest than it is at present.

"Not divided"! It must be nearly thirty years ago, I think, that St. Paul's, Lorrimore Square, was in the forefront of Anglicanism. There was a change of vicar, and the congregation so little realized that they were "one in doctrine" with their new clergyman, that a great part of them seceded, and formed the nucleus of what is now the large body of worshippers attending St. Agnes', Kennington. But why, if they were "not divided," if they were "one in doctrine," did they not stay where they were?

"Not divided!" Is not division the very essence of Protestantism? and are not the divisions in the Establishment sufficient proof that it is Protestant? "We have within the Church of England," said the Times on one occasion, "persons differing not only in their particular tenets, but in the rule and ground of their belief."

Put it another way. Take the case of a Nonconformist who desires to become a member of the Church of England: suppose him to be some one in this neighbourhood: is he to be taken to St. Paul's or to St. Alphege's? Who is to decide? Surely it is not a matter of indifference. Mr. Ruskin has said that "The Protestant who most imagines himself independent in his thought, and private in his study of scripture, is nevertheless usually at the mercy of the nearest preacher who has a pleasant voice and ingenious fancy."[1] And surely the Faith which is put forward as that of the Church of England, depends entirely on the belief of the individual parson referred to. How different is the case with the Catholic Church!

I have said that the Church of England neither has nor claims authority; and my last words shall be devoted to making this plain. If she has authority, as our High Church friends assert, whence does she derive it? Not from the old Church of England, for, by the Reformation of Elizabeth, the old Catholic episcopate was swept away. Of the sixteen surviving Catholic Bishops, all save one—Kitchin of Llandaff, who took no part in the Reformation, nor in the consecration of Parker—were imprisoned, and Parker and those consecrated by him were intruded into the sees of the imprisoned Bishops. But granting that Parker and the rest were validly consecrated, whence did they get jurisdiction? Certainly not from the old Catholic Bishops; most certainly not from the source whence these obtained it, namely the Pope; not by the fact of consecration, for orders and jurisdiction are distinct, and received independently of each other; not from any of Parker's consecrators—Barlow, Scory, Coverdale, and Hodgkins— for not one of these was in possession of a see, and they could not give what they themselves did not possess. The only answer possible, however unpalatable it may be to High Churchmen, is that they got jurisdiction from the Crown, or not at all.

Every Protestant Bishop now takes the oath of supremacy, by which he professes that the Sovereign is the "only supreme governor" of the realm "in spiritual and ecclesiastical things, as well as in temporal." Whence the Sovereign obtained this supremacy, or what "warranty of Scripture" can be adduced for it, I do not know; nor do I think it easy to ascertain.

Moreover, the Establishment not only does not possess authority, but she expressly disclaims it. The First General Council of the Church prefaced its teaching with—"It seemed good to the Holy Ghost and

---

[1] *Our Fathers Have Told Us*, III, 125.

26

to us": and the Catholic Church, right down to the present day, has spoken with like authority. But what does the Church of England say? Her anxiety not to be regarded as having any authority is almost pathetic: "All Churches have erred," says she, "in matters of faith," and it is implied that she may fail also. "The Church has power, indeed, to decree rites and ceremonies, and authority in controversies of faith, but it cannot decree anything unless it is taken out of Holy Scripture. General Councils are not only dependent on the will of princes, but, when assembled, may err and have erred, nor may the Church declare anything of faith which is not read in Holy Scripture." These things she tells us in her Articles of Religion. But, to go a step further, who gave Holy Scripture its authority? It claims none for itself as a whole; it nowhere tells us of what books it is composed; Christians are nowhere told to read it: no text bids us keep Sunday holy, or authorizes infant baptism, or the taking of oaths. Who vouches for the authority of the Bible, I repeat? Who but that Church which from the earliest times has been its guardian and its only rightful interpreter.

It is true that to claim authority is one thing and to possess it is another. If saying we had a thing were equivalent to having it, we should find nowadays authorized teachers in abundance. But it is difficult to believe that a body deriving its teaching power from God would take so much trouble to deny the possession of it. The Catholic Church does not act thus.

And when the spiritual head of the Establishment is consulted, he shows himself her true son. Some years ago, Mr. Maskell, who afterwards became a Catholic, asked the Archbishop of Canterbury, Dr. Sumner, whether he might or might not teach certain doctrines of faith? "To which," the Archbishop said, "I reply: are they contained in the word of God? Whether they are so contained, and can be proved thereby you have the same means of discovering as myself, and I have no special authority to declare."

Here is the judgement passed upon the Church of England by the learned Dr. Döllinger, a man who has some claim to respect from

Protestants, seeing that he had the misfortune to die outside the unity of the Catholic Church. "There is no Church that is so completely and thoroughly as the Anglican, the product and expression of the wants and wishes, the modes of thought and cast of character, not of a certain nationality, but of a fragment of a nation namely the rich, fashionable, and cultivated classes. It is the religion of deportment, of gentility, of clerical reserve. Religion and the Church are then required to be, above all things, not troublesome, not intrusive, not presuming, not importunate." "It is a good Church to live in," some one said, "but a bad one to die in."

The absence of authority and of definite teaching—these were the reasons which induced me to leave the Church of England. The step once taken, all was clear; and on every side I found abundant evidence that, if there be a Church of God upon earth, the Holy Catholic and Roman Church can alone claim that title. That evidence I cannot bring before you now—I have already detained you too long. My Catholic hearers do not need it, and my Protestant friends will do well to seek it from those better qualified than myself, qualified to speak with an authority which cannot attach to any sayings of mine. To both Catholics and Protestants I would recommend the perusal of the *Lectures on the Present Position of Catholics in England*, which were delivered by John Henry Newman, "the noblest Roman of them all," not long after he left the Establishment, thus, as Lord Beaconsfield said upon one occasion, "dealing the Church of England a blow from which she still reels." In those lectures you will find almost every popular objection against the Church met with a charm of literary style, and with a courteousness of expression which, so far as I know, has never been equalled; and even those who remain unconvinced of the truth of the Church will be constrained to admit that there is at least another aspect of things which seemed to them to admit of only one, and that a bad one. It has been well said that the truths of the Church are like stained glass windows in a building: look at them from without, all is confusion; but go inside, let the lights of heaven stream through them, and each fragment takes its place in the glorious and beautiful picture which is presented to your delighted gaze. So, from without, the doctrines of the Church seem dark and confused; but the light of heaven pours through them to those within.

THE ESSENTIALS OF
SPIRITUAL UNITY

Ronald Knox

THE ESSENTIALS OF
SPIRITUAL UNITY

PREFACE

When I began to be anxious about my position as an Anglican, I felt that I had no right to plunge into Catholicism (although I then held most of its doctrines) without going back over old ground, and satisfying myself that I had not unduly neglected the claims of other denominations to a hearing. Among other experiments in this direction, I began to write down some account of what I meant by "a Church." A Church I was determined to have, but it seemed to me it might clear my mind if I started with the bare idea and definition of a Church, and followed out the implications of that idea, wherever (as Plato says) the argument should lead.

My method was not that of Plato, but that of Aristotle, at least in his Ethics. For Plato knows what he thinks beforehand, and his dialogue form is a literary artifice, but Aristotle seems (at any rate) to set out on no other basis than that of generally received ideas—What do we mean by "good"? What do we mean by "deliberate"? and so on—and by whittling away the rival explanations that will *not* do, arrives in the end at the definition he wants. This nice slovenly method I adopted. When I found myself (as usual) "up against" the Catholic system, I exchanged this experimentalist for an *a priori* method, and began asking: If such and such a system of religious organization is the only tolerable kind of Church, how would such a Church (supposing it to exist) be likely to appear in the records of history? How much should we expect historical and geographical accidents to obscure, at first sight, the principles on which it was based?

The first part was begun as early as August, 1915, but the work went on slowly and casually, as the mood took me, and the last part was never really finished—the last page or two I actually wrote in September, 1917, just before I was received. I have let it stand as I wrote it, except for half a dozen incidental corrections which were suggested to me. I do not pretend that it is the way in which one ought to arrive at the idea of the Catholic Church; it is merely the way in which one soul did.

R. A. KNOX.

January, 1918.

THE ESSENTIALS OF
SPIRITUAL UNITY

1. The Church a selection, and one made by an agent from without.

The name *ecclesia* seems to postulate two points: first, that the body it denotes should be separated, *i.e.* there should be at least the human possibility of some people being outside it; second, that it is called, that is, defined from without, not self-appointed or self-determined, like a club or a republic.

2. And the principle of selection must be based on some qualities in those selected.

It is thus, in potency at any rate, exclusive. And since in an institution whose essence is concerned with matters of ultimate moment we could hardly expect the selection to be arbitrary, like that of a club, we must suppose the exclusion to be due either to the unfitness of certain people for membership on the ground of morals or belief, or else to the wilful refusal of certain people to join the institution, which would be, viewed from inside, the repelling of those who showed no aptitude for membership. Such unclubableness would be hardly human if the refusal did not base itself upon some tangible objection, an objection to certain qualifications which had been set up as tests for membership.

3. God selects, in the true sense, but this does not mean that man cannot know who have and who have not been selected.

It would be well to know at once who is the agent who calls out, and in what sense he does it. No form of Christianity would dispute that this agent is God: the difference would be that the Calvinist tendency, in so far as it is present in any view of the Church, makes the selection arbitrary (from our point of view), and based on pre-natal choice on God's part. But even supposing this to be true, the Church as a visible institution must have, if not merits by which its members are to be selected, at least marks by which they are to be recognized; and all Calvinist schools demand an immediate faith in salvation by atonement, most of them also a standard of practice consistent with such beliefs. On the other side, no Christian would claim that his embracing his creed was a matter purely of choice on his own part.

4. At least so far as a visible Church is concerned: there may also be uncovenanted mercies, with which we are not concerned.

In so far as God calls us, and presumably foreknows us, there is no inherent reason why we should expect to be able to say, This or That man has been called of God—so long as he knows his own sheep by name, all is well with their salvation. But if the Church is to be a visible institution, guarding common mysteries in its trust, or at the lowest binding people together in conscious fellowship, there must be marks by which they can be recognized. And here, it is almost universally admitted, we can take heart over the case of those who do not qualify for visible membership, yet puzzle us by the fact of their exclusion. God may have called them, but called them by special and uncovenanted paths; it is no business of ours on the one side to emulate, or on the other side to despair of them.

5. Underlying causes of non-membership must be: (α) some moral weakness, (β) some distortion of moral standards or (γ) some defect of speculative belief.

The actual formula which carries with it membership of the Church is not the explanation of anybody's inclusion or rejection; it is merely (if non-miraculous) the mark, or (if miraculous) the means of it. The explanation must lie in some determination of the man's own mind which is inconsistent with the terms of admission. Since there are to be no arbitrary or accidental qualifications, other than that the applicant should be a rational human being, the grounds of exclusion limit themselves to three.

(1) He may, though in theory prepared to accept the moral standards upheld by the society, fall so far short of them in practice, through *akrateia*, that the authorities judge him unfit.

(2) He may, through moral *akolasia*, or again through want of sympathy with particular determinations in detail of the moral code, be clearly incapable of entering into the spirit of the institution.

Or (3) There may be beliefs held by the society which he cannot admit, or *vice versa*. Some, no doubt, would prefer to see this last, doctrinal test abolished altogether, or at least reduced to a minimum. But in any case it must be reckoned with as a possibility.

Note—It might seem that there was a fourth possibility of disqualification, a disciplinary disqualification. The man might do and believe all that the members did and believed, yet refuse to put himself within a circle of like-minded people. But this, it will be easily seen, resolves itself either into a doctrinal or into a moral disqualification. Either he does not wish his own moral standards to be of universal application, in which case his practice is not in fact morally determined, but due to taste, preference, etc.; or else, admitting he believes the doctrines, he does not believe in the doctrines being vital, and in this absence of belief in his beliefs he is at variance with the members of the body.

6. The argument for (a) as the only obstacle appears logical, satisfying to moral instincts, Biblical, and traditional.

It might seem at first sight that (1) was, if not sole, at least of primary importance. For all sects agree that, whatever else is significant, moral action, which means precisely living up to the best standard a man knows, is of the very first importance. The Church would thus be a society of people united in the effort after individual perfection, and a man would be a member of it if and in so far as he achieved the standards required of him. This would seem to agree well with Saint Paul's language, when he refers to the members of the Christian community as saints, and insists upon charity, etc., as the true test of Christian character. It would also answer to our Saviour's own test, "By their fruits ye shall know them." If a man can be pronounced good he must, *ipso facto*, be pronounced a member of the Church, and qualified as the recipient of all its graces. Pressed to its furthest lengths, this argument would claim that all beliefs are a matter of individual conviction, and, precisely because they cannot conscientiously be abandoned or even suppressed to suit the convenience of others, they are not suited to form a test of admission. Pressed even further, it seems we should have to claim that differences of moral standard must meet with equal respect, provided they were not definitely underdeveloped, or demonstrably calculated to militate against the happiness of mankind in general or the society in particular.

And indeed, it is often supposed that the first concern of the Apostles was to keep the Church holy, rather than to keep it orthodox or uniform. The weapon of excommunication seems to have been used at first hesitatingly and with reluctance: the heresies Saint Paul combats might be said to have been condemned rather for their anti-social tendency, as putting a barrier between Christian and Christian, than for their false speculative views. Whereas the moral discipline of the Church seems to have been at its most severe in the early centuries: apostasy and adultery, certainly, were viewed so gravely that the author of them was, if not technically deprived of Church membership, at least debarred for life from the exercise of Church privileges. Logically, then, this principle can claim that in rejecting a candidate for membership, you are basing your action on a clear delivery of the conscience, a moral imperative, not on any point of dogma, not on any speculative question about which, after all, you may be wrong and he right. Sentimentally (to use the term in no unkind sense) it enables you to avoid the feeling that you are rejecting one who is in point of conduct just as good as yourself. Biblically, it corresponds with the emphasis laid on moral purity by our Saviour and his disciples. Historically, it seems to have much in common with what we know of the practice of the earliest centuries.

7. Until it is examined closely. Are we to admit people who live up to ANY standard, provided they do live up to it?

Preliminary objection to this view. It is clear, however, that there is a point at which it becomes rather difficult to draw the line between difference of moral standard and incompatibility of moral practice. The good Mussulman will have—or at least contemplate having—more than one wife; the good Hindu widow would till lately go further, and conceive it a moral duty to defy Christian standards in immolating herself over her husband's pyre; the Japanese, highly civilized in other ways, will commit suicide in grief at the death of their Mikado with the applause of their fellow-countrymen. It is true we describe these standards of morality as lower standards of morality; but are we sure we are not begging the question? They are at least positive standards, and they do clearly evoke a certain spirit of admiration in us, who have been otherwise educated. Would it be possible to have a Christian society in which two different Christians would conceive their duty, in the same given conditions, in diametrically opposite ways? Or, at least, would base their outlook on different views of the importance of human life, and the relative value of the two sexes? All this clearly suggests that the moral demands of a religious society are that its members should not merely live up, as far as possible, each to his own standard, but should own to some extent at least common standards. And the recognition of common standards in morality brings us suspiciously close to dogma.

To put the case in a more concrete and probable form: it seems doubtful if those Friends who are true to the spirit of their institute could fail to regard the bearing of arms against an enemy as anything but a total disqualification for membership. Yet there are Friends who have, in the present crisis, conceived it as not merely allowable but their positive and unavoidable duty to bear arms in this way. Each side is acting according to conscience, and it is very possible that some agreement will later be arrived at; but the agreement will mean the abandonment of one of the most cardinal principles of Quaker history, or at least its relegation from the sphere of moral duty to that of private conscience. In a divine Society, are such divergences tolerable? (In other denominations, the same difficulty does not arise, for though individuals or classes may feel debarred from fighting, they have no historical traditions against its legitimacy.)

8. Further, have we a right to judge motives? Can we be sure of distinguishing the penitent from the hypocrite? Discipline may be used in these cases, but exclusion is, precisely here, inappropriate.

But indeed there is a root difficulty, far more serious. We immediately become confronted with the problem of the moral struggle: "I find another law in my members," etc. It is quite certain that the Christian society exists to achieve the individual moral (and spiritual) perfection of its members, but is it certain that this end is best served by debarring the sinner *in toto* from communion? Is it not rather to be anticipated that the sinner will find means to triumph over his sins through membership, rather than by the fact of exclusion, which may easily induce despair or defiance in his attitude towards the body? Who is to distinguish between the case of the hypocrite who continually sins and continually feigns penitence, and that of the *recidivus* who constantly falls, yet disowns, and to some extent atones for his faults by genuine contrition? Is not he at least in a better position than the hypocrite who retains his membership by dint of not being found out, by secret sins and insincere confessions? Does not the example of the Friend of publicans and sinners rather suggest, that while demanding a penitent will on the part of the applicant for membership, we shall yet be indulgent to the sins against which he struggles, but not always successfully? In a word, is not the whole question of motives in action, and responsibility in moral cases, too complicated to decide by hard and fast rules of exclusion?

9. And the tendency to deal with the *recidivus* by kindness appears to be progressive.

Rightly or wrongly, this would appear to have been increasingly the practice of the Church, and under the influence of the Roman hierarch. So it was a Pope who stood out for the rights of the lapsed in the persecutions, and Pius X laid it down that Communion is too valuable a preventive against sin to allow of our dissuading the weaker brethren from its frequent reception. Whatever penances have been imposed, total exclusion has come to be reserved for those who are manifestly impenitent, since they will not abandon the sources of temptation; the harlot will not give up her means of livelihood: the man who has contracted an incestuous marriage will not live apart from his wife, and so on. In a word, exclusion is held to be justifiable only when immorality takes the form of moral obliquity, and the applicant for membership not merely fails to amend, but fails to admit even in theory the Christian standard of morals. We are thus forced back again from Class (1) of possible obstacles to communion, to Class (2).

10. We fall back then on the set of obstacles marked (β). But we find that (β), quite as much as (γ), excludes people from the Church on the ground of their conscientious convictions.

The difficulty then arises, whether Class (2) has any existence independently of Class (3). Or, to put it differently, whether for our purposes the two varieties of possible obstacles might not have been classed under the same head. For, as soon as you begin to talk of moral standards, moral values, or moral codes, you have passed out of the region of practice into that of theory. True, the theory affects the question "How am I to live?" but it is a theory for all that, because it is universal in its application. It might be said that it is at least not a matter of mere intellectual theory, for we speak of apprehending moral values, rather than making moral judgements; but this is beside the point in matters of religious discussion, for spiritual truth, like moral truth (if the term may be used), is a matter of values. All this does not affect the fact that a man may repudiate monogamy as he repudiates monotheism, as a matter of conviction, and complain, in the one case as in the other, that the Christian society is excluding him by reason of a conviction which he cannot help holding, because it alone satisfies his moral consciousness.

11. Resumption of preceding paragraphs.

It seems, then, that the Church, being a selection from among mankind, not an arbitrary selection, nor a hereditary selection (like the Church of Israel which it superseded), nor yet simply an assembly of good people (for motives, the tares in the wheat of the kingdom, are hard to disentangle, and good and bad must grow side by side till the harvest) must be selected, so far at least as it is a visible Church, on a principle of qualification which involves a common speculative outlook: it still remains for discussion, of course, whether this outlook need be only in the sphere of moral theology, *i.e.* in matters which affect actual conduct, or in purely speculative and devotional matters as well.

12. A body, which is human in its institution and in the promises which it offers, can include or exclude as it likes, because it is responsible only to itself.

In so far as any "church" or religious denomination is, as such, of purely human formation, the responsibility of deciding who is to be accepted and who rejected is almost intolerable—would be quite intolerable, but that such a society does not (or should not) profess to be the One Church of Christ; and therefore can, like any club or association, direct the disappointed applicant to some other society which is more likely to be in sympathy with his aspirations. But in so far as a church feels itself to be the One Church, and the guardian of certain divine privileges which, normally at least, can be obtained through no other means—to that extent, we must suppose, its authorities will be reluctant to disappoint any candidate, unless his disqualifications are such as have been declared by a supernatural authority to be necessary disqualifications. The sense of responsibility naturally operates in both directions: a society conscious that it is in the position, not of a plenipotentiary, but of a trustee, should be more careful as to whom it admits, not merely as to whom it rejects. Thus, undoubtedly, those religious bodies (the Congregationalists, for example) which claim no special divine charter, but merely the status of cultural associations, feel far more liberty in refusing or in accepting candidates for membership than, for example, the Church of Rome.

13. Is it possible that exclusion from the Church should rest on practical considerations—considerations, that is, of the exigencies of any society which is to have a corporate life?

We have, then, to consider the suggestion that religious tests should be insisted upon only where the failure to accept them would mean the failure to accept a common standard of behaviour necessary to the life and coherence of the religious body in question. Thus, the mere confusion which would be introduced into the social life of a monogamous society by the admission of a person with four wives might be held sufficient reason for refusing membership, without going into the question of ultimate sanctions. Or, again, complete incompatibility of outlook might be pleaded as a bar, if a professional soldier desired, without abandoning his profession, to be enrolled among the Society of Friends.

14. These considerations may be cultual as well as merely moral.

More than this, there may be cultual incompatibility which is not moral incompatibility. Thus, in a religious body whose members laid stress on "the gathering of themselves together" a man conscientiously convinced that all prayer was waste of time, who would consequently refuse to take any part in public worship, would clearly be out of place. Similarly, an observer of the Jewish Sabbath who refused to take any notice of Sunday might be rejected by a body interested in Sunday observance.

15. Answer to § 13: Yes, if the body be of human origin and value. No, if it be of divine. For a divine Society is too important a thing to be regulated by considerations of its own convenience.

But these purely moral and cultual considerations can be used as a basis of exclusion only if and in so far as the body in question does not profess to be of uniquely divine institution, and the sole true representative of fully-revealed religion. For their bearing, so far as we have hitherto considered it, is social only; and if the spiritual privileges forfeited by exclusion from the body are considerable, it becomes a question whether issues of social convenience should be allowed to weigh; ought not the weaker brother, for all his four wives and his refusal to attend church, be admitted to membership, if only as a weaker brother? It appears that he should, UNLESS THE TABOOS WHICH EXCLUDE HIM ARE OF AN ORIGIN AND A CERTAINTY NO LESS DIVINE THAN THE PRIVILEGES FROM WHICH EXCLUSION DEBARS HIM. In a word, a society of human foundation, guarding human privileges—a Benevolent Society, for example—is at liberty to reject applicants on grounds which claim no more than the sanction of human instinct or human theory —such a Society may, for example, exclude all except total abstainers. But a Society which claims to be of divine foundation, and to be the trustee of divine privileges, can exclude only where it has a divine sanction for excluding.

16. Instance of the difficulty here raised—the sanction of Sabbatarianism in the Church of England.

Thus even moral and cultual considerations can be considered a bar in the absolute sense only when their validity is guaranteed by the divine voice. The observance of Sunday in the Church of England is an interesting case in point. If the Church of England appeals only to Scripture, it is doubtful whether the observance of the first day in the week can be justified. If it appeals to the practice of the Church in former times, that is a different matter. But for a frank Erastian it seems it would be possible never to go to church on Sunday at all: he might regard the day as of purely conventional significance, set apart only by the action of the State, to the views of which he is not bound to conform; or, at best, by a consensus of ecclesiastical officials, whose injunctions, as being human injunctions, he may safely disregard.

17. A crucial instance resumed; why do Christian sects insist on monogamy? Not on any purely ethical ground, for such ground is lacking.

Let us take monogamy as a case in point. On what ground is a Church which claims divine institution to deny access to her privileges to the bigamist? It is very hard to say that the principle is part of the common delivery of the conscience of mankind; the Mahomedans sanction other practices, so did the ancient Jews—communities where we find clear recognition of the intimate tie between morality and religion. We cannot even appeal here to the equivocal term "progress": for in America monogamy nowadays seems to mean little more than the limitations imposed by Mark Twain on his pipe-smoking. The Utilitarian test, always doubtful in this connexion, breaks down absolutely in face of a great war that stamps out a large part of the male population. We might say that in Europe it has become part of the recognized principles of society, and could not therefore be abrogated without infinite confusions; but even this return to the practical appeal would be nugatory in those African countries where society at large tolerates the principle of the harem, and those who desire to become Christians find great social difficulties in consequence. We must have a divine utterance to support us if we are to incur the odium of insisting on this particular taboo.

18. In this case, it appears, we are bound to invoke a supernatural authority: and if we have once invoked it, we are henceforward its servants, wherever it chooses to lead us.

That is to say, we must invoke an authority. And in doing so, we must see clearly what we are doing. In order to plead an authority here, we are submitting to the dictation of our authority (whatever it may be) on all subjects on which it may choose to dictate—not merely on all matters on which we find it convenient to appeal to it, for this is clearly destructive of the very essence of authority. It must be such that we cannot say "I do not agree with it here"—for, if not, our friend with the four wives will ask us to take no notice of it in his case either. In emancipating ourselves from the indecisive rule of King Log— practical convenience, etc.—we are electing King Stork. In appealing to the bramble for a ruling, we are making it king of all the trees,—not for this or that occasion, over this or that issue, but at all times and everywhere alike: with it, not with us, rests the decision as to how far it will carry us.

19. Three possible groundworks of qualificatory beliefs; reducing themselves to two: (1) A written contract, (2) a living voice.

It does not appear that any religious system has ever appealed to an authority which was not expressed in one of three ways:

(1) By supernatural illumination accorded to individuals, generally in moments of prophetic exaltation.

(2) By the written word, which is really a variant of (1), since it implies illumination granted to an individual (or set of individuals) the content of which has been committed to paper. In some systems the revelation once given is closed for all time; in others, it is capable of being supplemented by fresh illumination accorded later.

(3) By certain powers of inerrant judgement vested in an individual or set of individuals and guaranteed to operate only when such and such conditions are unfilled. It seems clear that any such succession of individuals demands some process of co-optation, in order to insure that the empowered officials C and D are the legitimate successors of A and B.

Reduced to this logical absurdity, principle (1) would mean simply "one man one church." The people who quote the text "All thy people shall be taught of God" do not make this claim, but it is doubtful if they ought not to. If, contrary to Saint Paul's assumption; all were Apostles and all Prophets, a Church like that at Corinth might divide itself, not simply into followers of Paul and followers of Cephas, but into a number of sects equal to the number of those who had been members of the Church: each regarding the illuminations accorded to himself as of paramount authority, and excommunicating the rest if and in so far as they disagreed with himself. We might have supposed, of course, that a miraculous consensus of opinion would be granted to all who earnestly ask the guidance of the Holy Spirit, without further ado; but the history of Christendom does not fortify us in this opinion.

As a matter of fact, private inspirations are more usually claimed by a large number of people for some one person of special spiritual gifts; if the content of this revelation is sufficiently startling to make the disciples disown, or be disowned by, the religious body from which they started, the new inspiration, in passing into an institution, necessarily comes to base itself either on the principle of the Bible or on that of

47

the Church. Either the original founder's words are carefully treasured in writing, and, while susceptible of expansion or of interpretation, are not considered susceptible of alteration or correction; or else a succession of prophets has somehow to be guaranteed, mediating a succession of divine illuminations adequate to any emergency that may arise. We can, in fact, have no quarrel with private inspirations as such—they have been granted to St. Gertrude, St. Teresa, Blessed Margaret Mary, etc.—they do not in reality form a distinct basis of authority until they become the foundations either of a new Bible or of a new Church. Thus we can neglect the first of our three headings; and say that only a Bible or a Church, or some compromise between, or combination of the two, can give us the authority which we find necessary to the delimitation of a visible Church.

20. Whether *a priori* or on grounds of experience, it is difficult not to suppose that a religious body, however much it professes to be purely Biblical in its standards, must fall back on some kind of living authority, if only for interpretation.

The difficulty would naturally occur to us, even if we had no history for our guide—What is to happen in the case of a religious body avowing a Book as its sole source of religious authority, if two sections of thought should disagree as to the way in which this or that document should be interpreted? The only solution of such a problem seems to be, to go to law before the unbelievers, and appeal to a purely commonsense tribunal to decide whether faction A or faction B is truer to the letter of the title-deeds. But, although this may be a necessary step where temporalities are concerned in the dispute, it is obviously an expedient to which any religious body would have recourse only with the greatest reluctance, as in the case of the U-Free and Wee-Free controversy. For, if there is any meaning in Saint Paul's contrasts between the letter and the spirit, if there is any truth in his contention that the spiritual man has the sole right of interpreting spiritual things, then it is clear that the value of such an appeal is purely a matter of convenience. No, if there is to be any uniform standard of belief, even supposing the original Message to have been delivered in the clearest terms of which human language is capable, a situation is humanly speaking bound to arise in which two rival schools of interpretation will wish to submit their differences, not to a mere arbitration, but to competent judgement. Since the written letter stands, judgement must be pronounced by some person or body of persons conceived as divinely commissioned to issue a decision. Divinely commissioned, because a mere *consensus theologorum*—and a consensus of this kind is not easily arrived at—would not be accepted by the losing side, who would plead that if the matter were purely one of intellectual conviction, their own failure to see eye to eye with the pundits could not fairly be held to disqualify them for communion. It is unnecessary to elaborate historical instances which illustrate this tendency on the part of every body to appeal to some sort of authority, however vaguely it may in some cases be conceived: probably only very new religious bodies, such as the Irvingites or the Christian Scientists, have escaped such difficulties.

21. Whatever therefore be avowed as the ground of belief, the definient authority from time to time must be a living voice.

It is perfectly possible for a man, asked why he believes this or that, to say, "Because the Bible says so." His Bible or Koran may be the ground of his faith. But if he be challenged with the question, Why do you believe this rather than that, when the Bible seems to admit of two possible interpretations? He must appeal to some living voice which has, however vaguely, defined the doctrine in question. This is presumably the substratum of meaning which underlies the very misleading catchword, "The Church to teach and the Bible to prove." Whether, in this case, the definient authority does not become also the ultimate authority, is a difficult question, but does not concern us here; it is enough for our purposes that any religious body may be forced, and must be prepared to be forced, to produce an authority for what it holds in common, even on questions of morality: this will probably be the fate of most religious bodies soon on the cardinal problem of the dissolubility or indissolubility of the marriage tie.

22. The principle of One Man One Vote does not solve the problem of authority.

However excellent the purely democratic principle may be in a country or in a fictitious institution such as a club—the principle, that is, of counting heads to avoid breaking them—a "poll of the members" does not seem to be an expedient often adopted by religious bodies. The reason is not difficult to find. A majority may have a right to decide on a purely practical point—*e.g.* whether seats should be free or rented—in matters where only the well-being of the body as a human society is concerned. But if the problem be, not to arrive at the will of the society, but to arrive at the will of God, it is not to be wondered at if an appeal to the vote leaves the minority unconvinced and prepared for schism. "They are slaves who dare not be in the right with two or three." We have no divine guarantee that the voice of the people will be the voice of God: rather, we must be prepared to expect that in any society which is not violently rigorist, the majority will be largely composed of people whose spiritual insight is not of the keenest.

23. A variation of the popular principle—the Conciliar theory.

There is, however, a variation of this theory which, discredited as it is now, appears to have commended itself to solid thinkers—the Tractarians. This is the pure Conciliar theory, according to which certain representatives of the body, meeting in conclave, were actually prevented by the overruling influence of God from arriving at a false conclusion. Such a body is not representative in the strict sense; for even if all the members of it had been popularly elected, it was still not in virtue of their election, but in virtue of a special gift *ab extra* that they were preserved from error. The difficulty of this doctrine is twofold.

24. Difficulties of the pure Conciliar theory.

(1) It does not seem to be claimed by any tradition of the Church that our Saviour himself attached any promise of infallibility to such gatherings. Nor does the Church seem to have acted on the understanding that a decision of this kind was necessarily final. There were still Judaizers after the Council of Jerusalem in communion with Christians who rejected their views, though the tendency to sever communion was constant. Further, Irenæus knew well enough who were heretics and who were Catholics at a time when there had been no ecumenical council since that of Jerusalem: are we to suppose that infallibility resides equally in each of a number of local synods?

(2) We should surely have expected that, if this miraculous guidance was to be bestowed, there would always be an overwhelming majority in favour of the right side, if not complete unanimity. Yet we see that at various periods rival doctrines could claim very nearly the same number of upholders among the Bishops.

25. A more modern Conciliar view.

The Conciliar doctrine therefore seems to have undergone an amendment in recent times, and the decisions of the Councils are now claimed as binding (or something like it) not on the ground that the Councils were directly inspired, but on the ground that the Church, by no sudden show of hands, but by slow processes of assimilation and rejection, came to hold one view or the other, and so ratified the decree. Such a view can at least claim texts such as "He shall guide you into all truth," "All thy people shall be taught of God," etc. And it does not seem difficult to suppose that God has implanted in the hearts of those who endeavour to keep the unity of the Spirit an infallible tendency towards, or instinct for the truth, which, like the red corpuscles of a healthy body, ejects naturally the invasions of alien doctrine. Such a view is also very comfortable at the present day. For, if we are prepared to look upon the ecclesiastical history of the last four hundred years as an interlude, and to call by the name of Christian all those who seriously claim the title, we can console ourselves with the hope that perhaps after all the questions raised at and since the Reformation are only specially gristly mouthfuls, which the Church is slowly taking her time to digest; nothing is settled as yet, but being all Churchmen we shall inevitably, in the end, come to see things in the same light. Probably this view is held, in one form or another, by almost all Christians outside the Roman and Eastern churches who are seriously exercised about the question of Church unity and Church authority.

26. This view seems to put us back where we were before.

This doctrine, in the form in which it has become popular among Nonconformists and laxiorist Anglicans, is destructive of the whole principle of a visible Church or an audible authority. For, if we believe what we believe about the Trinity, not in obedience to formulas laid down at Nicea and elsewhere but because "Christians" have in course of time come to believe such doctrines, and found them suited to their religious needs—then we must be prepared to revise those beliefs in conformity with what "Christians" are coming to believe or may come to believe about the Divine Nature, fortified now by methods of criticism wholly different from those of the Fathers. Nothing has been defined, nothing ever will be. The "churches" are but a number of philosophical sects within "the Church," holding various but equally tenable opinions on almost all points—whether the Unitarians are to be counted among these, and if not, why not, seems at least a legitimate speculation. Anybody is at liberty to revive the principles of the Agapemonites without forfeiting his title to Christian membership. The One Visible Church, if it ever existed, only survived by a few years its Divine Founder, and can expect a renascence only in the remote future, when prayerful application to historical documents shall have produced a basis which we all feel conscientiously bound to accept.

27. A refinement of this doctrine seems to confound its own supporters.

There is, however, a refinement of this doctrine commonly held among more rigorist Anglicans. According to this view, although the Church does make up its mind, not by sudden Conciliar illumination, but by a gradual process of assimilation, yet the doctrines once so assimilated have become "defined," and therefore irreversible (however much they may admit of interpretation). The Church may make up her mind, centuries hence, on such a point as the withholding of the Chalice, or (from their point of view) the Immaculate Conception, but what has once been scaled, in the early ages, is sealed for ever—*e.g.* the marriage laws, the three Creeds, the three orders of the ministry, at least two Sacraments, etc. Since the schism between the East and the West the Church has been unable to formulate any opinion which "counts," seeing that she has been divided.

But we must press for an answer—Do we hold such and such doctrines to be of faith *because* the Church has come to believe them, or *because* they have been defined by Councils? If the former, then what right have we to assume that the Church has finally made up her mind on (say) the doctrine of the Trinity? Why should the process of doctrinal development have petrified? How are we to distinguish between kernel and husk, between what in traditional belief is part of the *depositum fidei* and what is merely accidental and suited to the needs of an age? We fall back once more on private opinion to determine this, which it does with no certain sound. If on the other hand we say that the Councils are the defining voice, but we accept them not in so far as they spoke in the heat of controversy, but in so far as they registered beliefs which by their time had become unquestioned: if, that is to say, the controversy on circumcision was really settled at Nicea, and the controversy on Arianism at Constantinople, and so on—then indeed we avoid all sceptical difficulties about "snap votes," "undue influence," and the like, but are we really better off? There still remains the objection that we have no proof that a majority can define

53

a generally accepted doctrine, any more than decide a controversy with the assurance of Divine ratification.

28. We are, in fact, still left with a circular argument, or a bare confidence in numbers.

In fact, whether it be the continuous history of the Councils, or the continuous history of the Church at large, to which we appeal when we say that this or that doctrine is irreversible, we are still arguing in a circle. Asked what is the Orthodox Faith, we say, "What was and is believed by the Orthodox Church." Pressed as to what the Orthodox Church may be, we fall back on defining it as the body which holds the Orthodox Faith. And if all the Episcopal Churches of the world were re-united to-morrow, and had a schism the day after, we should be reduced to voting with the majority: this view is supported by *n* prelates—*Dieu le veult*: that view is supported by *n*-1 prelates—*A.S.* And even then we should have to admit sadly that it was left for our grandchildren to know which party was in the right.

29. Logical outcome of the Divided Church theory.

If anybody is disposed to rest content with the view that all appeals for authority should be made to the early and united Church, or at best to a consensus of opinion between the Church of Rome and the Orthodox Churches of the East, he has still to face this difficulty—namely, that if such an appeal be made by either means to an undivided Church on the question, Can the true Church of Christ lack the signs of visible unity and union? The answer would surely be an unanimous chorus of "No." In which case we are confronted with an authority which does not even believe in itself.

30. Logical outcome of the bare majority theory.

If on the other hand we are disposed to treat the schism between East and West on a line with all other schisms, and say that the fragments it left constitute (i) a true Church and (ii) a schismatic body:

then, whatever the precise numerical proportion of bishops, it is difficult not to feel that the West has it, as representing more different countries, more active thought, more vigorous life. And we are thrown back on a merely platonic Gallicanism, which (however) insists that the bishops of the Roman communion met in council are infallible: and if we admit that, then in obedience to them we must admit the whole Roman claim.

31. Logical outcome of pure *consensusfideliumism*.

Nor do we escape the *impasse* by appealing from episcopal councils to the general sense of the great body of Christian people. For the great body of Christian people, unless we are prepared to suppose that anyone who now claims the title of Christian is necessarily a member of it, must in some way be defined, and the only conceivable definitions of it (if we are taking our stand on historic continuity with the sub-Apostolic Church) would be (i) the Church of Rome or (ii) the Orthodox Churches of the East. Not both at once, for the faithful of either rite disown the company of the other. Here again, if we set aside the kudos which, since the division, has accrued to the Orthodox Church through the rise of the political power of Russia, could any casual observer fail to find the true *fideles* in the communion of Rome— more especially when we remember how intimately the doctrines of the Greek Church seem to have been bound up with those of the reigning Emperor, long after the Church in the West had become, corporately at any rate, independent of such influences?

32. Especial claim to a hearing of the Roman Church if we take the *consensus fidelium* basis.

The salient difficulty of any *consensus fidelium* theory is surely this, that if the test is to be a real test the term "*fideles*" must have a definite meaning in extension. And while we look in vain for any other definition of their extent which will not be a *merely* circular definition, the Roman Catholic has a ready answer: "The *fideles*, be they many or few, be their doctrine apparently traditional or apparently innovatory, be their champions honest or unscrupulous, are simply those who are in visible communion with the see of Rome." No doubt in the long run this means the people who are so orthodox that Rome has seen no reason to excommunicate them, so that unity and orthodoxy still react upon one another: but the fact remains that the Roman theory does give a test for defining the *fideles* without the question-begging preliminary of ascertaining who the *fideles* are, from an examination of their tenets. And in fact there can be little doubt that in the West our labelling of this party as orthodox and that as heterodox in early Church history comes down to us from authors who were applying this test of orthodoxy and no other, and that we, at the Reformation, made our appeal (in so far as we did make any appeal) to the Churches of Jerusalem and Alexandria, meaning thereby not the Nestorian or Monophysite claimants to these sees, but the representatives of the body (hence admitted as "Orthodox") which had remained longest in communion with the Roman Church.

33. The difficulties of principle, which produce these logical results, investigated.

All Conciliar theories of the Church (except those which at once fix an arbitrary limit to the number of the Councils, neglect the question, "Whence do the Councils derive their authority?" and apparently blind themselves to historical phenomena) seem on examination to labour from a single root defect—they attempt to define the Church by the Faith, not the Faith by the Church. They posit the faith as a known quantity: it may be simply the Swanwick test, belief that Jesus is God: it may be the doctrines (roughly speaking) of the Judicious Hooker: it may be the Council of Trent: it may be anything betwixt and between. But in any case you posit the faith as a known thing, defining it by an arbitrary standard, and then say, "Who are there who believe these doctrines? They are my brothers." True, you may insist, in questions like that of Ordinations, that the faith shall be attested by corresponding ecclesiastical practice, and even that this practice can show continuity (what of the Swedish Church, for instance?), but in any case you assume that Catholicity is something that you instinctively know, and can apply as a test to any religious body you examine. By this means you accept the Greek "Orthodox" and the Old Catholics, while you reject the Nestorians and the Presbyterians. For this is (except on the narrow Conciliar view above described) what you are doing when you speak of "orthodox" and "heretical" tenets in Early Church history. But how, apart from pure Bibliolatry or miraculous revelation, are we to know what is the minimum of belief and practice that can be called Orthodox, unless we have One visible and continuous Church to teach us on the point? How much more satisfactory, if the Church were a body which leapt to the eye, self-credentialled, so that we could posit *it* for our starting-point and infer from *its* teaching what was true and what was false!

34. If there were a single Church, designed to be the standard of the Faith (and not vice versa), how should we expect it to be constituted?

It may be following an idle fancy, but it is surely not altogether presumptuous, to blot out history as far as possible from the mind's eye, and imagine how we should expect the one, indivisible Church to be constituted, so as to be a safe guardian of the Faith.

We should expect that either a single body of men, kept in close touch with one another and divinely guaranteed against serious doctrinal disagreement, or (better still) a single man, since in the last resort it is the casting vote that counts, would be selected from among the immediate followers of the Founder, who in the last resort would be the safe camp to pitch your tent under. Let us suppose a single man. We should expect that such a man would be open to advice, even (if he seemed to be hesitating in following his conscience) to reproof from the highest officials round him. That, as the first missionary work was done, while the Founder's words were still fresh in men's ears, and his

57

chosen disciples yet alive, little recourse would be had to such a man, or indeed be geographically possible. That while disagreements would be few, in that blessed sunrise (except perhaps in connexion with some who from the first had misconceived the scope of the whole enterprise) these disagreements would be dealt with locally, on their own authority, by other officials who saw their duty clearly: that the malcontents in these cases would attempt to plead the authority of the absent X (let us call him) and that the official they were opposing would (while insisting on his own exceptional knowledge of the Founder's intentions) be occasionally at pains to show that his views did not differ from—perhaps even were instrumental in forming—the views of X. That X would be divinely guided to make the headquarters sooner or later at Y, the most prominent or most central city of the then known world, where he would very likely be associated for missionary purposes with that official whose task it had been to organize most of the churches on the way to Y from their original starting-point, and that the churches more immediately under the care of this official (Z) would be in close contact with the Church at Y. And now, what happens at X's death?

35. Transmission of the centralized authority.

We might think it probable that X would nominate and solemnly appoint his own successor, guided in his choice by the same infallible assurance which would make it impossible that he should take the wrong side in a doctrinal dispute. But this is to assume that the gift which makes him what he is a sort of habitual grace, which can only be conferred by him who already possesses it. If, on the contrary, the gift were rather in the nature of an actual grace, conferred according to a covenant *on condition of* his holding a certain position, but not in and through the act of his elevation to that position, then the appointment might be left to others. Not, in such geographical conditions, it is evident, to the whole Church. The appointment can safely be made in such conditions and by such electors as would be common in the ordinary election of the officials of the body in local cases; for the gift which determines his special character being a *charisma*, which overrules (presumably) any natural tendencies in the man which would unfit him for his special office, could be bestowed on any candidate thus appointed, even were he not "the best man in." It would not be unnatural to suppose, in fact, that the providential character would be conferred on the man whom the Church at Y selected as its head (the bishop, let us call him): they elect and enthrone him, and God immediately bestows *ab extra* the special grace needed for a special position.

[There are other ways, clearly, in which the thing might be managed, but in the absence of a claim on the part of any other succession of persons to a Caliphate of this description, this way of managing it would seem a very natural one.]

36. Early centrifugal influences to be expected.

We should expect that while the congregations in various parts were poor, scattered, and persecuted, there should be little intercourse between the Church at Y and those elsewhere (although it would naturally be mentioned with some deference, when mentioned at all). That the Church, rather than the Bishop, would be the object of respectful allusion, since (1) his power derived from his position, (2) the local Church was more of a distinct unit when converts were few, (3) the Bishop himself would be likely to live in some obscurity, owing to his exposed position in times of persecution. That we should not find him interfering in the affairs of other churches except those within a fairly easy radius by sea. That when local quarrels arose, they should be settled by local councils, especially while men were alive who had had speech with the immediate followers of the Founder— it would rather be the innovators who would seek, and would fail to find, recognition of their doctrines at Y. That old-established or central congregations would naturally come to exercise a sort of local satrapy over other congregations around them. That bishops of great learning, or such as had showed great courage in persecution or sanctity of life, would be more prominent to the ordinary eye than an official living at a distance. That minor differences of usage would crop up between various churches, that Y would become involved in them, and that Y's first attempts to make regulations of ecumenic force would be resented, and that recriminations would come from both sides where matters of old-established usage were concerned. That if the Bishop of Y seemed to be exercising his presidential prerogative with undue assertiveness, he would be remonstrated with in impatient language. That he, as having the interests of a wider community at heart, would take a gentler and a less rigorist view on matters of discipline than the officials of outlying churches.

37. Effects of State recognition on the Churches.

If it should so fall out, that the chief temporal power in the world should come into the hands of one who was at least sympathetic with, if not actually committed to the principles of this Church, he would naturally be concerned with the settlement of any disputes that might arise; in the case of a considerable dispute, it would be he who would facilitate the travels of officials from distant parts to a single centre, and be present at the discussion in the person of his representatives to secure "a free field and no favour" in times when bluntness of speech and hastiness of temper were not unknown in high ecclesiastical circles. If the Bishop of Y should, in virtue of the importance of his see, be unable to be present in person, it is possible that his legates would not occupy the chairman's place, which would be given (no doubt with the Bishop of Y's sanction) to another bishop of high standing.

Human nature being what it is, it is only natural that this temporal authority should at times be wielded by persons who attempted to exercise a direct influence on the councils of the Church; by intriguing for the appointment of this or that candidate for vacant sees, by "summoning" councils in unrepresentative geographical conditions, etc. Owing to the force of the secular arm, the candidate favoured by such a ruler in a given case would be likely to gain the temporalities of the see, and the dispossessed candidate, were he right or wrong in his views, would appeal from this secular compulsion to the Bishop of Y. The secular ruler would therefore make every effort to influence the views of the Bishop of Y; would, in an extreme case, persecute him, and try to wring from him a decision against his conscience. If and in so far as such a decision should be given under the influence of (i) physical force or (ii) insufficient information, or a combination of the two, then it would be right for those who looked to Y for guidance to stick to his previous and uninfluenced judgements, rather than to any extorted profession, as the norm of right belief.

If the secular authority should build a second city, intended to outstrip Y in dignity, it would be natural that the Bishop of this new city (C) should, if worldly-minded or ambitious, try to set himself up as in some way on a level with the Bishop of Y. If the secular empire should then be divided between Y and C, the Emperor of C would be all the more inclined to support the Bishop of C in such pretensions. The bishops of churches nearer C than Y, accustomed to rally round the Bishop of C as their patriarch, might easily come to be more overshadowed in practice (without justification in theory) by the Church at C than by the Church at Y; and law-abiding citizens, in the event of a schism in the Church at C, might be tempted to support the candidate backed by the Emperor of C, without troubling much to enquire which candidate was supported by the Bishop of Y. This process, though contrary to the original intentions of the Founder, would take place by insensible stages and largely without conscious revolt: only at times of open breach between the Bishop of Y and the Emperor of C would the case definitely present itself to the conscience—Is it to be God or Cæsar? For so long as, and in so far as, the churches accustomed to look to C for a lead were united by the unity of faith with the Bishop of Y, they would be rightly called "orthodox"; but at whatever periods they supported the Bishop of C against the Bishop of Y they would be formally disobedient, with whatever excuse of deficient information, etc.: if at any time a definite and formal breach took place, the party however large or important, which sided against Y, would be guilty of formal schism. And however faithfully henceforward they guarded the deposit common to the Churches of C and of Y, they would nevertheless be cut off from the unity of the Church.

BACKGROUND

James Britten gives an attractive picture of growing up in an Anglo-Catholic parish in the late nineteenth century; he is less eirenic describing the violent differences he found in other Anglican churches. For Britten, the sheer contradiction between Anglicanism's professedly unsacramental evangelical Protestants, and the pastiche Catholicism of its ritualist clergy destroyed its claim to be the proper branch of the Catholic Church in England.

Where Britten had been a sympathetic lay participant in Anglican ritualism, Ronald Knox was one of its clerical spearhead. His whole effort in the decade before the Great War had been to make the Church of England live up to what he saw as its rightful Catholic heritage. The pain he felt when, in the midst of the loss and uncertainty of the War, he realised he was no longer convinced by his own arguments, can be clearly seen in his memoir *A Spiritual Aeneid*. Here, however, his presentation is wholly dry and analytical.

CTS ONEFIFTIES

1. FR DAMIEN & WHERE ALL ROADS LEAD · *Robert Louis Stevenson & G K Chesterton*
2. THE UNENDING CONFLICT · *Hilaire Belloc*
3. CHRIST UPON THE WATERS · *John Henry Newman*
4. DEATH & RESURRECTION · *Leonard Cheshire VC & Bede Jarrett OP*
5. THE DAY THE BOMB FELL · *Johannes Siemes SJ & Bruce Kent*
6. MIRACLES · *Ronald Knox*
7. A CITY SET ON A HILL · *Robert Hugh Benson*
8. FINDING THE WAY BACK · *Francis Ripley*
9. THE GUNPOWDER PLOT · *Herbert Thurston SJ*
10. NUNS – WHAT ARE THEY FOR? · *Maria Boulding OSB, Bruno Webb OSB & Jean Cardinal Daniélou SJ*
11. ISLAM, BRITAIN & THE GOSPEL · *John Coonan, William Burridge & John Wijngaards*
12. STORIES OF THE GREAT WAR · *Eileen Boland*
13. LIFE WITHIN US · *Caryll Houselander, Delia Smith & Herbert Fincham*
14. INSIDE COMMUNISM · *Douglas Hyde*
15. COURTSHIP: SOME PRACTICAL ADVICE · *Anon, Hubert McEvoy SJ, Tony Kirwin & Malcolm Brennan*
16. RESURRECTION · *Vincent McNabb OP & B C Butler OSB*
17. TWO CONVERSION STORIES · *James Britten & Ronald Knox*
18. MEDIEVAL CHRISTIANITY · *Christopher Dawson*
19. A LIBRARY OF TALES – VOL 1 · *Lady Herbert of Lea*
20. A LIBRARY OF TALES – VOL 2 · *Eveline Cole & E Kielty*
21. WAR AT HOME AND AT THE FRONT · *"A Chaplain" & Mrs Blundell of Crosby*
22. THE CHURCH & THE MODERN AGE · *Christopher Hollis*
23. THE PRAYER OF ST THÉRÈSE OF LISIEUX · *Vernon Johnson*
24. THE PROBLEM OF EVIL · *Martin D'Arcy SJ*
25. WHO IS ST JOSEPH? · *Herbert Cardinal Vaughan*